bootlegging apples on the road to redemption

mary elizabeth grace

INSOMNIAC PRESS

Copyright © 1995 Mary Elizabeth Grace

Edited & designed by Mike O'Connor

Copy Editors: Phlip Arima
                     Lloyd Davis
                     Liz Thorpe

Canadian Cataloguing in Publication Data

Grace, Mary Elizabeth, 1965-
        Bootlegging apples on the road to redemption

Poems.
ISBN 1-895837-30-8

I. Title.

PS8563.R33B66 1995   C811'.54   C95-930201-8
PR9199.3.G73B66 1995

The publisher and the author gratefully acknowledge the support of the Canada Council through the Explorations Program.

Printed and bound in Canada

Insomniac Press
378 Delaware Avenue
Toronto, Ontario, Canada
M6H 2T8

for my mother and her eyes
for my father and his hands

"We are words made flesh"

— Leonard Cohen

"now there are no bonds, except the flesh but listen, it was
Thursday, there was this boy Manzini ..."

— Gwendolyn MacEwan
Manzini: Escape Artist

"I will arise and go now, and go to Innisfree,
And I shall find some peace there for peace comes dropping
slow."

— W.B. Yeats

ೆ

I'm not even going to attempt to name your place in this
book's life. Thank you.

Mike O'Connor, Waheeda Harris, Elizabeth Otto (Labagh),
John, Peter, Michael, Alex, Noel Whelan, Marvin Hinz,
Carrington, Larry Nuesbaum, J. Rupert Ritchie, Rob Glen, Lisa
Elaschuk, Phlip Arima, Ferris Argyle, C. Derrick Chua, Joan &
Sandor Molnar, *Poetry, Pomegranites and other Passions* (Jen
Haberman, Zaf Gousopoulos).

Photos in the text were taken by Elizabeth Otto, Carrington,
J. Rupert Ritchie and M.E. Grace.

If I had known
that such a place existed
that place before breath becomes air

I would not have believed myself
such a broken, brave child.

I would have listened twice
I would have heard your crying
in the middle of my crying night.

such a place existed

Bootlegging Apples on the Road to Redemption

I stopped at the side of the road for awhile
My pennypram was weary and so was I.

It was then
I saw him.

He must have been standing there for more than a few minutes,
for he had mud on his face and mud on his precious white linens.

Well I started pulling the waist of my skirt up to my ribcage,
the way I always did when feeling courageous around a stranger.

And so I asked him,
yes, himself, Jesus,
I asked him what he thought of all this?

I must admit,
he looked angelic in all his willingness.

But I still felt compelled to make it perfectly clear,
in fact I spoke rather impatiently.

You do understand this is completely illegal?
He looked at me, sorta dazed
I was beginning to think he wasn't the Christ child
but a simpleton with bruised blackberries for brains.

And he kept smiling down into the carriage, as if looking
into the hope of a small face, not a heap of stolen fruit.

But then he took an apple from the pram
Started making it shine with his soiled hands.

It was then he spoke, and I swear to God it was the truth.

Course,
I know what I heard could have all come from the plain
fact I'd stopped eating sup these days past.

The bites of an apple just kept getting caught in my throat
it's like it didn't matter, the flesh or the core,
every time I started to swallow I started to choke.

So, maybe I'll quietly go to hell for blasphemy
Maybe I'll be celebrated, stoned to death with a bag of potatoes
Maybe it was just my hunger that made me see
him that way, made me hear him say
Whatever keeps blood out of the baby's bottle is my only prayer.

— for the Moore Street women, Dublin

Cut-and-come-again-cake smile

Agh

She's a Killeybeg's girl
with a cut-and-come-again-cake smile

She wore a black jack rasta rat-ta-tat hat

She said she fell in love with a rave boy from Jersey
'cause even though he was a foreigner he gave
good *craic*

But then one day
he came in
said it was his things
he was packin'

said he was finding it hard
to appreciate
her
kind of beauty

she let him go
no flesh torn

She had enough years to understand
sometimes it's best to shoot that black crow
before it's born

so she sat herself down
to a fine dinner
even dipped her tongue into the rose of sherry

afterwards
she took her mother's family tartan

cut it up into strips
braided her hair
then
used those ribbons
to knot the spoon, fork and cork
all in
and
here's me
prayin' over words
never gonna be
half the poet
she

just is

craic: Irish slang for a good time

— *for John, Finn and Uisce's Shoot the Crows*

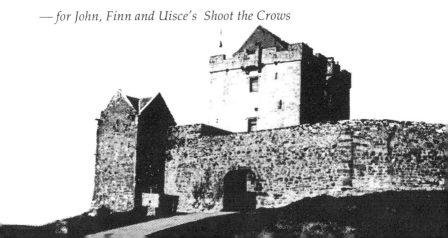

A Boast to Kavanagh

Remember when Kavanagh would take his walks, come out of his thatch-roof door, said all that bending forward is what kept him humble to his gift. He'd place himself on those rose and leaf rocks, Jesus they looked like marble in some great music hall with him sitting there like that.

He'd close his eyes, breathe slow and deep. Sometimes it wouldn't take very long, other times, it would take one hell of a long time. Heard him in the pub saying he had to wait until the sea was in him; I'm not kidding you, that's what he said and he had tears in his eyes when he was saying it. Said he knew it was in him when his heart started flapping like the wings of a strong bird. Yeah, I remember watching him raise that violin with one tight twist of the wrist. Heard him in the pub saying he'd rub the side of his face into the curve of it, until the wood was as warm as skin. I'm not kidding you, that's what he said and he had tears in his eyes when he was saying it. Said he did it for the woman he never got to love.

Christ he was an Irishman. Remember that music. We got to hear what the sea sounded like if it was a violin, or was it the other way around? I forget how he used to say it. Agh, just shut the hell up. None of you are goddamn listening anyway.

— for Bev and Kevin

Tomorrow to Donegal

down to Donegal
down
down to Donegal down

you and I friend

down to Donegal
down
down to Donegal
down

You and I friend

down to Donegal
down
down to Donegal
down

you smile
still easy with my one-day wish to sing
(and no sense of direction)

— for Labagh

It Behoooves Me

It behoooves me, all my bewailin'

I say

I want a bag of brand new bones

I do

I'm going to take meself to bounty store,
bring me home a pound or two.

In fact, I'm going to put them on right there,
walk out proud as if I'd just bought meself a brand new
pair of shoes.

It behoooves me, all my bewailing

I say

I want a bag of brand new bones

I do.

Saint Sweeney

Sweeney Sweeney Sweeney

Saskatoon two-step
with key-lime eyes
doing the Sycamore shuffle
across Syracuse bridge

patio lanterns making me think of tall pink lemonade
looking a little out of place
in this sky's blizzard

What am I trying to say?
Am I reaching for the fantastical, mystical, inspirational?

No,
it's just the first snowstorm of the year
and it's my way of coping with cabin fever
and someone telling me lyricism is dead

Jo Jump Ride

I'm going to jump the Jo Jump Ride and take it, take it, take it down the tracks

I'm going to jump the Jo Jump Ride and take it, take it, take it down the tracks

Where Alden and I would spend the whole night dancing, coming up with our own jigs. They always ended up being 1 part wit and 2 parts O'Reilly's famous spit & swig.

Where Alden and I would spend the whole night laughing, leave in the morning, the world amok with the mayhem of our song.

Where Alden and I would spend the whole night talking, as if we had something to say, thinking ourselves the new poets, we were living our prayers.

Where Alden and I would spend the whole night lying on our backs, getting stoned on open sky. For him everything was there, all our screaming was all our screaming, he never heard the seagulls squawking.

Mulberry Sleeve

I said
she had her own story

you smiled your slow steady Russian roulette
smile that always kept me running, past remembering,
past ever being at peace with what was,
what is

I said
this time I'm going to change things

I'm not going to find myself with my back against some wall
somewhere that doesn't matter,
shouldn't matter, only matters
because you've decided
to visit

I said
she had her own story

mouth an overgrown strawberry, tangerine hair,
sad, sullied, indigo eyes that would have had
van Gogh asking forgiveness

You turned
unravelled your long mulberry sleeve
wiped the sweat of my brow's betrayal

quietly said

everyone is granted that one nobility

I Have Stumbled

I have stumbled twice
once for love and once for life

At seventeen
if I had told others of my passion

they would have said for worldly things
I was far too keen

I didn't tell them, for they would have been wrong

It was my love of godly things in worldly things
I was, some would say, far too keen

So on that day
I heard the old woman talking outside my father's shop

I made myself drop the keys
for the caution in their voices made me curious

Ah but fate, but fate, but fate,
her face has yet to greet the boy of Bauheen Moor

They say his other island skin wears the dark brown
of ten good harvests

Ah but fate, but fate, but fate,
her face has yet to greet the boy of Bauheen Moor

They say the light green of his eyes
could grant the world its dream, or be the giver of its demise

Ah but fate, but fate, but fate,
her face has yet to greet the boy of Bauheen Moor

It was enough for me
these few words

I went home saying I was to visit my sister's place

I walked four nights
I walked four days

And it was in the clearest hour of sun's giving
just before taking back all its hope
I thought I saw his face
but I couldn't say for sure

For it was in that moment my step faltered
and I stumbled twice upon Bauheen Moor

And so alone
unable to move I fed upon the flowers
colours that held me in a trance
as if staring down into the darkness of a well
but this time
I was staring into different shades of light
and for the first time
I had no want
of hearing my name call back to me

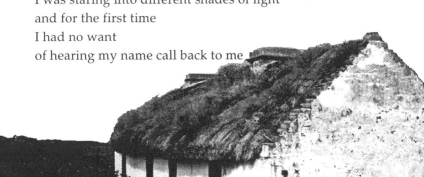

Eventually my broken bones healed, I was able to stand,
although I was never able to walk to lower ground

So this is where I've spent my life
making dyes
became talked of for the colours
I coveted and coaxed from flowers

and I'll admit
I am proud of this small thing
those who've walked this way
have walked in my same passion

You're probably wondering why I am telling you all this

You,
a mere stranger, in want of some new colour

It's because I'm coming to that time, becoming child again
getting ready to walk innocent into some new life

And two things stop me from telling a priest
One, I dye my blacks well so it's years before the church need
come this way again

Two, I am an old woman alone
there is no mirth or mayhem in listening to my story
there would be nothing for them to take back
nothing gruesome, nothing of glory

as I said, myself I cannot walk down
besides, there is little I miss
except on certain nights

I will suddenly wake, walk out

all is quiet

the wind carries up the water and if I part my lips
just a little I can taste the salt of the sea,
but then it's as if my sight gets jealous of my taste and
starts me crying

Crying for him.

I'll admit he's not at all forgotten.

In the daylight
I will sit upon my stool
lean my back against my humble slant
and say to myself
as I watch a new colour drying in the sun

"This time, this time, this time
it has been done

this is the colour, the true light of his eyes

This time, this time, this time
it has been done

This is the colour, the true dark of his skin."

I know
in telling you my life's secrets
what brought me here
what made me stay

You could call me fool
it was just a story, words not even meant for me

Others would say
one's destiny is always one's virtue deceived

I say
Pshaw, pshaw
this is my place, this is my place

Down the Road

I believed my soul
to the gypsies down the road
in exchange
I was given
a kerchief spread vulnerable
and a pocketknife that made me bleed.

Shantytown Girl

I took my three names and walked out of the rubble, the remembrance,
the regret that was my life, into the rituals of my own civilization,
realizing it was only my soul I could save.

Shantytown girl
with Shantytown eyes

How many years have you been biding your truth
living other people's lies

How many years have you listened to them tell you
if you plant and water something it will grow

Well there is no growing
when the ground is concrete
and the only garden is
four brick walls

Shantytown girl
with Shantytown eyes

— for Michael

Someday

Somedays
I get so tired of all the misunderstanding
I get so tired of all the anger
I get so tired of all the pain

Somedays I'm walking forwards, somedays I'm walking backwards. Somedays all I'm doing is falling down. Somedays I know I'm looking faith in the face. Somedays I'm close to crawling and it just keeps walking away.

Somedays
I just stay inside my room
I'm scared of the wars inside my head
I'm scared of the wars inside other people's houses
I'm scared of wars inside countries I don't even know the names of

Somedays I see an old woman smiling and I know she's still loving her old man. Somedays I see a little boy with tomorrow in his eyes and I know someone's been telling him today's a good place to be. Someday I hope to find the courage to get to that other place that's something better than this 'cause there's got to be something better than this.

Contempt

I'm afraid
my heroes have lost their courage tonight

they will settle for the comfort of the fire
idly discuss my life
as if they really care

(they know enough
not to put so much effort into existence)

we sit in the other room
chatting
not comprehending the worth of a life, imagined or otherwise

Requiem

mind goes, mind falters, I am beyond any understanding that
doesn't belong to this moment, even in this my world sunders, my step
stalemates, so many ideologies trampling through my head scribbling
their red ink, in that one room I had hoped for solitude, a place to carve
one's name into one's bones, leave them there, hoping for some new birth

What I Want — Ode to Immortality

What I want, is what I want, and what I want, is what I can't have.

What I want, is what I want, and what I want, is what I can't have.

The oyster is open, two halves broken.

The sand of me runs through my hands, no pearl of it to be made.

The epiphany is called Rage.

What I want, is what I want, and what I want, is what I can't have.

Beggar's Bounty Wish

Scar tissue, not string, binds another's truth
wings,
the middle pages

rip them out

      let them scatter

        on the floor

there,
   that is me

        gathering feathers

wanting   more

Bring Me Brave

The babbles and the babes
bring me brave
to this far, far place

Covering me in the purple of promise

It is the unknowing of the known
that makes me weep
makes my want to bury myself
in this dark earth
become need
the desire to feel for the first time clean

The babbles and the babes
bring me brave
to this far, far place

Covering me in the purple of promise

before breath becomes air

September Never Coming

I asked you to cut me flowers from the soon-to-be-September fields.
I asked, because I thought it would please.

Instead, you brought me the head of a dead man
spoke of the greatest gift being to teach one
of another's grief.

I asked you to bring me a pale pink dress.
I asked because of need.

An attempt at beauty,
something to cover these bones
that, still assembled in this order,
make my body.

Instead, you brought me the bowl part of a broken cup
to catch the dripping of my blood.

This is Today

when he was a boy
he knew a summergirl with grey eyes

when he was a boy
he knew a summergirl with grey eyes

even before they met
he believed in the mist

he would wake early
sit close to the river
watch the different images
as they walked out of the water

every year she came
every year he made a different bracelet
for when she left

until he was fourteen

in this moment
he takes a grey stone
wets it in the river
buries an edge in the grey ashes

the paper says
he is the one who understands the language
he must mark things as they are

the people say
he is the one who understands beyond language
he must mark things as they are

he repeats to himself
This is today, This is today, This is today

hoping the Shaman's words
will make him believe
yesterday he was not old enough to see the faces

We Came Slow

We came slow
to your stone house

You had my same name
I had your same age

We spent the day in the kitchen,
talking of small things —
the coming of winter, the changing of the windows,
the way your little boy, when tired of tall people's talk,
liked to run outside and count angel's wings

We sat, watched you make scones and drank tea
We sat, ate some scones and drank even more tea
We sat, ate all the scones and drank all the tea

I remembered watching you
thinking about what your brother said
When you first moved to the farmhouse
your husband would take the palm of his hand,
brush it against your ear
to make the sound of the ocean
it was the only way you could sleep those first few years

My only regret of that day was not having the chance to see
the two of you in one room together

I had gone to bed early
you and your brother stayed up talking late
he came in,
whispered into my hair
she said we are blessed with the same rage

I turned
two minutes, two hours,
it doesn't matter
response in darkness seeks its own time

I said,
you must have told her everything

He said,
I didn't tell her anything

Today his letter tells me you are dead

I take comfort in knowing my love for you
had come easy in that first and only time we met

but I can't let go of the red-soaked dream screaming in my head
of your little boy running into the kitchen, it empty

Mommy, Mommy, you said there were angels in the sky

Mommy, Mommy, you said there were angels in the sky

Who is this God

What is his lie

— *for Mary Whelan Kelly, Noel and family*

Lilan Loves her Lilacs

Lilan loves her lilacs
loves them with a face so true

She believes,
if she throws her marbles and pennies high enough,
lilacs will come dancing down to her

When that day arrives
I'll be there to witness all her believing
gather those flowers up in my arms

Plant her a garden, perhaps two or three
maybe then,
she'll give that lilac love to me

Gypsyleafgirls

Autumn wind,
We praise you far too much.
You are simply a naughty schoolboy
Wanting to lift the bright swirling skirts
of all the gypsyleafgirls.

Second Sight

She
walks up to me
willow trees, green apples, peppermint leaves
I say you look so clean
she turns away
thinking I haven't seen her for who she is

— for Sarah and Sean

Russian Doll

Angels do not live in heaven
they sleep in the eyes of my children

the devil does not wash his hands
with the stones under our feet

he lives in this house
he comes to my kitchen
he washes his hands at my sink
with my white soap

holds my children
as they dance and sing for him
their mother

Shouldn't it

Shouldn't it come easy
I'm not talking about making love
I'm talking about words

Shouldn't it come easy
or should I have to stutter

Same imagined knife
its tongue tracing thick veins

Shouldn't it come easy
I'm not talking about making love
I'm talking about words

Shouldn't it come easy
or should I have to silence

Same imagined knife
slow
steady
curious
to taste
the boiling point of blood

Shouldn't it come easy
or should I have to hold still

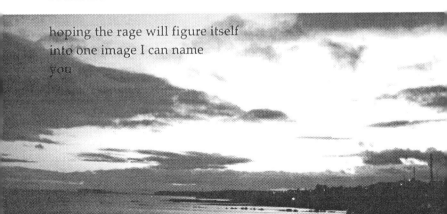

hoping the rage will figure itself
into one image I can name
you

Degas Damned

it was your smile
rim of a slender glass
full of waiting water

Macaroon Smile

The man with the macaroon smile,
often smiles,
at me,
telling me lies,
which make me believe,

I will be a queen one day,
of some,
far gone,
escaped place,
from which I've left no name,

Says,

like tracing the rings of a tree

in my eyes
in my eyes
in my eyes

— for Nik

Anon, Anon, My Sweet Shay

I broke a heart once, what seemed like a long time ago.
It was my love of his land, that made me love him so.

Dark hair, green eyes, Yeats' painting of parson's smile.

He said I was his "Maud Gonne."
Would I be his bride?

Anon, anon,
here are the words I spoke to my sweet shay
for his heart was of a younger kind.

These waters might be more yours than mine, friend
but you still have a lot to learn about the coming of the tide.

Despite my answer, he was still generous in offering
the moss of his moors
and the green of his grass.

In return, haughtily I let him feel pain and shame for not knowing
how to make my heart beat fast.

Now
three years have walked
between us
not three words exchanged
but I wish to return.

Yet I've come to understand,
if one wishes to journey in their own bed
they must first be able to sleep.

Such is not the case for me;
there is an image my mind too well keeps.

Me, walking
the moss of the moors
the green of the grass

Calling his name and him not answering back.

The calling
    turns to weeping
            and the weeping turns to flood

Such that heavy with water becomes the hem of my full skirt
I try to gather it in my arms, but I find no strength.
I twist
    I turn
        I drown in his good earth.

In part, he was too young.
In truth, I was younger yet,
to believe it would be another kind of love, not his,
which would cause me such regret.

I broke a heart once, what seemed like a long time ago.
It was my love of his land that made me love him so.

Anon, anon, my sweet shay...

Hummingbirds and Ghosts

I chanced upon
a picture once
that told me
there is a connection
  between hummingbirds and ghosts.

So I sit in my faithless hours
wishing the same wish —
that I had enough brilliance to see
the connection between mishap and myth.

The connection between
me and my chapel-hands mother
me and my prophet-bound father
me and my looking-glass brothers.

Perhaps if I choose my memories correctly
I shall remember,
the hummingbirds and ghosts
 were an abstract line on a page.

I contrived their existence
I conceived their connection.

Bayou Dream

It was once said
or perhaps it was me
waking from the damp of a bayou dream

When you see the light in someone's eyes
it is a darkness turned inside out

like the streetlights
shining on the face of an old man
as he spends the night pacing his one room
still wearing his winter coat
terrified of his last sleep

Hair Ribbons are only for Heroes' Daughters

I sat
watching him in the corner
hand trembling
combing his hair for the first time in twenty years

I sat
watching him in the corner
hands becoming fists
trying to get strong
for what I knew I'd see in his eyes

Shaman Lust

The first
I heard your name
I knew you were

like the story ...

I didn't need to know.

The Shaman believes
life exists
somewhere in between
it is never one or the other
it is what makes the soul dance in a circle
it is what makes the drum beat louder

Like the story of the man who waits for his lover to return,
she doesn't until the leaves are gone, all that time he doesn't
speak,
has kept his gift of blackberries safe in the boat of his tongue.

— for Jen

your crying in the middle of my crying night

Hush of the Bliss

I come collected of things yet to be gathered

My words do not comfort or curse
but drop from my lips
berries that have lasted
the winter long
by the bridge.

From the crushed raspberries of my mouth
they will drop into the pottered
bowl of broken bliss.

I ask myself what I write of, what I seek
all
I seek is beauty,
a sweet simple truth to gather up in the arms of myself,
a believing.

A hush,
to subdue
the strong, tortured carryharp
that leans in the hollow of my chest

Don't ask me where it came from
it was born in the curve of me
rough hewn,
aching for that one thought
to make it smooth.

Blackfly Wedding

A friend of a friend told me
you will be wed in the place to the place

I collected raspberries in mason jars
sat on the swing chair of the front porch

all their deliciousness weighing heavy in my lap
will this become memory

twenty-five years

all I know of answer
belongs in image

the silences
curled in my chest
an old bird
its wings the pale green curtain
in that timber house that last summer

today
wanting light
I spread them wide
cloth crumbling in my hand

OhmyOmagh

We'll spend the day in Omagh, Omagh, Omagh
where oh my
the boys talk so soft and warm
If I were a butterfly
in a green and purple storm

I'd go to Omagh, Omagh, Omagh
where oh my
the men talk so soft and sweet
If I were a butterfly
in a green and purple storm
their mouths
is where I'd want
my wings to keep

— for Martin and Tony

Wedding Vow

I will cradle you in the autumn of your aching.

I will carve the last good fruit out of its skin,
make a canopy for you to lay
your crimson leaf fevered head.

I will collect your tears
that drop like the scattered pearls of a madwoman,
carry them in my back pocket even if it means years.

Until one yellow morning,
you will see me for who I am.
I too am naked in my
knowing, waiting for you
to remember we kissed once.
It has been a gift. Taking
the singe of death from our
tongues.

Crossroads Cant

I just can't seem to jive with so much of this big town,
same as that small town kinda style

I just can't seem to funk for very long with any of these boys
next door

my Job, my Papa God, my Jesus, my Messiah, my Buddha
ain't got just one face

I'm tired of the rhetoric, the intellectual, the patriarchal of
empty rant and rave

It hangs, a dead rat in my face

Just give me some soul, some words with flesh,
something to do with the magic, the macab(re)

Just give me some soul, some butter to spread smooth and sexy
on this day's bread

— for Sadnar, her soul poetry and the borrowing of her "Papa God"

Brother Love

north, south, west, and east
the map without you
only a sheet
of paper

when that day comes
I'll know
either
one of you
or I
has left this place

— for John, Peter, Michael, Alex

Deep Song for Celia's Own Love

Mother loved me for my Spanish eyes;
said they made her believe in history
for the first time.

Brother loved me for my lopsided grin;
said he could tell his teachers
there is at least one thing that doesn't have an explanation.

Sister loved me for my long hair;
said it was smooth, combing it
kept her from being bored on Sunday afternoons.

Father loved me for the way I could hold his secret
in the palm of my hand
and no one heard it screaming.

*Deep song is very intense, emotional Spanish music associated with
Andaselian gypsies. Deep songs are often songs of resignation.*

Harmonic Rasp

You play a *czardas*
with that hand
those two fingers half gone

that the child in me says never belonged

except
to some black and white photograph
in some history book
about some war
that
has never
lived
in my head

will we ever sit
at the same kitchen table
agree
the pain they caused you
equals
the pain you caused me

it doesn't matter
it's all red
it's all mixed blood

it's just you and I
you playing your harmonica

the grey now coming into your dark hair
the grey now coming into your dark eyes

czardas — a Hungarian dance with a slow start and a quick, wild finish.

Seashell

When we promised
I saw
me tying a ribbon to your wrist
you tying a ribbon to mine

running
ribbons reaching
laughing

glass, stones
crushing
beneath us

at night
we'd sit

let the water
lick the blood

take its colour
paint our lips

me making you woman
you making me warrior

fall asleep in the womb of a seashell
not being afraid of each other's other

Visiting the Sorrow Tree

I must go back to all the places
we had been together

I must sit at that table,
I must sit under that tree

I must sit and let the hours pass

Ignore the waitress,
ignore the leaves

Make grotto of my grief

Sabbath of Our Love

Everything has told me twice.

You shall come to me today wearing a sorrow
that has withered
the fields of heather
that are your lovely eyes.

A sorrow
that talks of the fury
in an old woman's prayers
the forgiveness in an orphan boy's cry.

And I shall kneel in front of you
ask how it is
I can make tender your tattered wings
so once again
all they shall know is flight.

And in your quiet way
you shall continue
tying white rag ribbons to the juniper tree
murmuring
again
and again
in a voice
that makes the cloth of my skin
rip open
vulnerable to all that you feel
again

and again,
I will hear
shh,
there is nothing for you to beg of me
just promise to be near
and know,
these are for the sabbath of our love.

Pagan Passion

The brown of your eyes are the black-eyed suzies
that always grow wild.

The dark fire of your hair is the cinnamon and chicory root
that always burns in summer's midnight air

They say the truth will be sullied by my spoken word,

let it be done

for it is your Canterbury smile
that brings out my pagan passion

Your presence evokes

I don't know whether to laugh or to cry

You make me believe that the world has just begun

Olé

You know, by the way she moves she's had the cool joy
of wading in the waters of her own flesh

she stomps her foot

heart pounds heavy at the promise of thunder

she raises her head

limbs turn liquid at the promise of flight

I'm wrong
she is all of sea

Madda Madda Rose

The church bells ring across the street at St. Mary Magdalene's, corner of Manning and Ulster, and this still-unfamiliar landscape of sirens and streetcars fades away as the promise of redemption repeats itself. I guess it doesn't matter where you live, all realities seem to fade away against the promise of redemption.

It's true

> There's a certain kind of peace sleeping next to a church even though I'm still searching for my own kind of prayer

It's true

> There's a certain kind of peace sleeping next to a church Mary Magdalene, Babylon Bride, Jesus Lust as its saint

It's true

> There's a certain kind of peace

But this morning, early November morning, I wake before the bells begin, hours before the bells begin. I stare at the bare branches reminding me of bones, old age, death, and the concrete cross against the slate sky offering a heaven and immortality isn't any kind of comfort.

But it's an early November morning waking into the unspoken, place of no words only wanting words, kiss wanting curse, curse wanting kiss
I wait for them

Church bells clang
Sound breaking the air
Same crazyjoy when you smash
a coloured glass
against
the wall

Church bells clang
Sound breaking the air
Same crazypain when you smash
a coloured glass
against
the wall

glass,
colour your heart
turns
when it's breaking

Madda Madda Rose
I place my high cross on you high

Madda Madda Rose
I place my high cross on you high

It's an early November morning waking into the unspoken
place of no words, only wanting words, kiss wanting curse,
curse wanting kiss

moment into memory into moment
into memory into moment

You'd wake
> whispering words I didn't understand, didn't need to
> understand,
> notes singing into me, comfort of a lullaby

You'd wake
> understanding I didn't want to know about your love,
> love is a choice,
> voice moving into me, my belly burning, a prairie fire

We'd fall asleep
body against body
like
word against word
simple, powerful magic

I'd wake
> into the unspoken
> place of no words
> only wanting words
> kiss wanting curse
> curse wanting kiss

Times when lullaby, prairie fire didn't bring me back familiar
Chaos of thoughts, images and feelings choking on words

> barn swallows screeching
> from the heat and dust of vision
> thick and blurred
> always imagining,
> never surrendering,

throats torn silk
crashing into
epiphany

(and somewhere
a crippled soothsayer
offers a blessing
in exchange for a night's
shelter in a beehive,
steals a satchel full of honey
when he leaves, hibiscus
guiding him out of the mist)

I seek no shelter that offers refuge

I'd wake
    into the unspoken
    place of no words
    only wanting words
    kiss wanting curse
    curse wanting kiss

    Chaos taking my courage
    and all I craved
    was skull
    against stone
    clean straight line of pain
    mind tracing it
    serenity found

(somewhere
a child in a peacock-
coloured dress
is reading Braille,
word first touch)

I do not believe in sanity from being alone

moment into memory into moment
into memory into moment

He said
My body belongs to you

I remember tracing his tattoo
it was a boat and inside it a man and a woman
were holding each other
the mast was a harp

I said
It was beautiful

He said
It wasn't his

I said
You are what you love

He said
You are what you hate

moment into memory into moment
into memory into moment

He said
Don't kiss me, breathe me

everything went black

I tried again
stared into his eyes
green turning to blue
blue turning to lavender
exploding in my head
a purple flower

I laughed and told him the story of how when I was a kid I'd
spend a lot of time reading, waiting for the perfect moment to
do a little ecstasy
I'd picked a lavender flower, lay on my back, took one of the
petals, put it on my tongue and hold the flower in my hand,
and if I could stay still and stare at the flower long enough this
feeling would come and the purple would explode into white
peace
You laughed and said I was lucky I didn't try it with valley
lilies. I never tried it with white flowers, the feeling I wanted
was white, how was I supposed to get there if that's where I
started?

I'd watch you
body slow with sleep
strong, sure of its one dream

I wanted to wake you, but was scared you'd look at me the way
my mother did, when I'd sometimes smile her mother's smile.

She'd suddenly start to cry, laugh or get angry, looking through me, prophesying my life, and I'd end up yelling back,

> take a second look mother, I'm old enough to be
> my own story

I'd leave mumbling, the only thing I remember of her were the rosary beads, and that's only because it's the first time I saw lavender

I'd never wake you
(for that answer)
I'd watch you
body slow with sleep
strong, sure of its one dream

You say
The one you love today
is a memory of me

I forgive you for your poetry always could, always have,
English is your second language

I forgive you for your poetry always could, always have,
always have had to justify this struggle
for sanity for not knowing what colour white and white makes

Madda Madda Rose
I place my high cross on you high

Madda Madda Rose
I place my high cross on you high

These words
a haunt
in my head
half-hero, half-hunger
singing out of me

These words
a haunt
in my head
half-hero, half-hunger
singing out of me
like
ragheart serenade

not knowing a goddamn thing about my life

me
only
wanting
a
purple
petal
on
my
tongue
a
purple
flower
in
my
hand

no words

only
the

white

of
ecstasy

exploding
in
my
mind

It's true
I'm still searching for my own kind of prayer

Madda Madda Rose
I place my high cross on you high

Madda Madda Rose
I place my high cross on you high

— *for Andre, still wishing you all colours of purple*

Other titles from Insomniac Press:

The Last Word: an insomniac anthology of canadian poetry
edited by michael holmes

The Last Word is a snapshot of the next generation of Canadian poets. The poets who will be taught in schools, voices reflecting the '90s and a new type of writing sensibility; writers who have been taught and respect the current generation of poets, but are forging their own styles and distinction. The anthology brings together 51 poets from across Canada, reaching into different regional, ethnic, sexual and social groups. This varied and volatile collection pushes the notion of an anthology to its limits, like a startling Polaroid. Proceeds from the sale of *The Last Word* will go to Frontier College, in support of literacy programmes across Canada.

5 1/4" x 8 1/4" • 168 pages • trade paperback • isbn 1-895837-32-4 • $16.99

Desire High Heels Red Wine
Timothy Archer, Sky Gilbert, Sonja Mills, and Margaret Webb

Sweet, seductive, dark and illegal; this is *Desire High Heels Red Wine*, a collection by four gay and lesbian writers. The writing ranges from the abrasive comedy of Sonja Mills to the lyrical and insightful poetry of Margaret Webb, from the campy dialogue of Sky Gilbert to the finely crafted short stories of Timothy Archer. Their writings are a dark, abrasive place populated by bitch divas, leather-clad bodies, and an intuitive sense of sexuality and gender. The writers' works are brought together in an elaborate and striking design by three young designers.

5 1/4" x 8 1/4" • 96 pages • trade paperback • isbn 1-895837-26-X • $12.99

Beds & Shotguns
Diana Fitzgerald Bryden, Paul Howell McCafferty, Tricia Postle, and Death Waits

Beds & Shotguns is a metaphor for the extremes of love. It is also a collection by four emerging poets who write about the gamut of experiences between these opposites from romantic to obsessive, fantastic to possessive. These poems and stories capture love in its broadest meanings and are set in a dynamic, lyrical landscape.

5 1/4" x 8 1/4" • 96 pages • trade paperback • isbn 1-895837-28-6 • $13.99

Playing in the Asphalt Garden
Phlip Arima, Jill Battson, Tatiana Freire-Lizama, and Stan Rogal

This book features new Canadian urban writers, who express the urban experience — not the city of buildings and streets, but as a concentration of human experience, where a rapid and voluminous exchange of ideas, messages, power and beliefs takes place.

5 3/4" x 9" • 128 pages • trade paperback • isbn 1-895837-20-0 • $14.99

Mad Angels and Amphetamines
Nik Beat, Mary Elizabeth Grace, Noah Leznoff, and Matthew Remski

A collection by four emerging Canadian writers and three graphic designers. In this book, design is an integral part of the prose and poetry. Each writer collaborated with a designer so that the graphic design is an interpretation of the writer's works. Nik Beat's lyrical and unpretentious poetry; Noah Leznoff's darkly humorous prose and narrative poetic cycles; Mary Elizabeth Grace's Celtic dialogues and mystical images; and Matthew Remski's medieval symbols and surrealistic style of story; this is the mixture of styles that weave together in *Mad Angels and Amphetamines.*

6" x 9" • 96 pages • trade paperback • isbn 1-895837-14-6 • $12.95

Insomniac Press • 378 Delaware Avenue
Toronto, Ontario, Canada • M6H 2T8
phone: (416) 536-4308 • fax: (416) 588-4198